PRINCEWILL LAGANG

Threads of Success: Unraveling the Business Genius of Amancio Ortega and Zara

First published by PRINCEWILL LAGANG 2023

Copyright © 2023 by Princewill Lagang

All rights reserved. No part of this publication may be reproduced, stored or transmitted in any form or by any means, electronic, mechanical, photocopying, recording, scanning, or otherwise without written permission from the publisher. It is illegal to copy this book, post it to a website, or distribute it by any other means without permission.

Princewill Lagang asserts the moral right to be identified as the author of this work.

First edition

This book was professionally typeset on Reedsy.
Find out more at reedsy.com

Contents

1	The Rise of a Visionary Mind	1
2	The Fabric of Innovation	4
3	The Marketplace Tapestry	7
4	The Customer Connection	10
5	Chapter 5: Innovation and Adaptability: Zara's Enduring...	13
6	Threads of Reflection: Unraveling the Zara Phenomenon	16
7	Beyond the Seams: Charting the Future of Fashion and...	19
8	A Tapestry Unfinished: Continuation of Zara's Journey	22
9	Threads of Inspiration: Zara's Influence on Fashion and...	25
10	Threads of Continuity: Zara's Enduring Relevance	28
11	Threads of Reflection: Lessons and Insights from Zara's...	31
12	Threads of Inspiration: Charting Your Own Success	34
13	Summary	37

1

The Rise of a Visionary Mind

Title: Threads of Success: Unraveling the Business Genius of Amancio Ortega and Zara

The air in La Coruña, a small coastal town in Spain, carried the whispers of change in the mid-20th century. It was in this quaint setting that Amancio Ortega, a young man with a glint of ambition in his eyes, began his journey into the world of fashion and business.

1.1 Early Days in La Coruña

Amancio Ortega's story is one that begins with humble origins. Born into a modest family in 1936, he spent his early years observing the ebb and flow of life in La Coruña. The narrow cobbled streets and bustling markets would unknowingly shape the foundation of his future empire. As a teenager, Ortega took his first steps into the textile industry, working at a local shirtmaker's shop. Little did he know that these seemingly ordinary experiences were weaving the threads of an extraordinary success story.

1.2 The Seeds of Entrepreneurship

As the 1960s dawned, Amancio Ortega's entrepreneurial spirit blossomed. Fuelled by a vision that transcended the local market, he co-founded Confecciones Goa, a small bathrobe manufacturing company. This venture marked the inception of Ortega's keen eye for market trends and his ability to transform ordinary garments into coveted fashion statements. The threads of his success were being woven meticulously, one innovation at a time.

1.3 Zara: A Vision Unveiled

The turning point in Ortega's career came with the establishment of Zara in 1974. The brand, born out of a desire to revolutionize the fashion industry, embodied Ortega's philosophy of fast fashion and affordable luxury. Chapter 1 explores the strategic decisions that led to the birth of Zara, from its innovative supply chain model to the emphasis on in-house production. Through meticulous research and interviews with key figures, we unravel the threads that bind Zara's success to Ortega's genius.

1.4 The Quilt of Fast Fashion

Fast forward to the 21st century, and Zara stands tall as a global fashion powerhouse. Chapter 1 delves into the intricacies of the fast-fashion model pioneered by Ortega. The seamless integration of design, production, and distribution, coupled with a rapid response to market trends, set Zara apart. We dissect the quilt of strategies that allowed Zara to not only keep pace with the ever-changing fashion landscape but also dictate its direction.

1.5 A Glimpse into the Genius

Threads of Success offers readers a glimpse into the mind of Amancio Ortega, the maestro behind Zara's triumph. Through anecdotes, interviews, and a thorough analysis of his business strategies, this chapter sets the stage for a comprehensive exploration of the man who redefined the rules of the fashion game.

As we unravel the intricacies of Amancio Ortega's journey, the narrative threads of success become increasingly visible. Join us on this captivating exploration of entrepreneurship, innovation, and the indomitable spirit that propelled Zara to the summit of the fashion industry.

2

The Fabric of Innovation

Title: Weaving Tomorrow's Trends: Zara's Innovative Design and Production

In the intricate tapestry of Zara's success, Chapter 2 delves into the very fabric that defines the brand – its innovative approach to design and production. From the drawing board to the showroom, Amancio Ortega's vision for Zara revolutionized how the fashion industry approached creativity and manufacturing.

2.1 Designing the Zara DNA

The creative heartbeat of Zara pulsates in its design studios. This section explores how Zara's design process sets it apart. We investigate the collaborative efforts of in-house designers and external trend-spotters, uncovering how Zara manages to balance innovation and commercial viability. The chapter unveils the secrets behind the creation of collections that capture the zeitgeist of each season while maintaining Zara's distinctive identity.

2.2 The Agile Production Pipeline

Zara's success is not solely attributed to its designs but also to its unparalleled agility in production. Chapter 2 examines the intricacies of Zara's unique production model – a system that allows the brand to move from concept to shelf in record time. From cutting-edge technology to just-in-time manufacturing, we unravel the threads that ensure Zara remains at the forefront of the fast-fashion phenomenon.

2.3 Fast Fashion's Environmental Tapestry

As the fashion industry grapples with sustainability concerns, Chapter 2 scrutinizes Zara's environmental footprint. How does the fast-fashion giant balance the need for speed with ethical and environmental considerations? We explore Zara's initiatives in sustainable fashion, from eco-friendly materials to recycling programs, and evaluate the challenges and successes in weaving an environmentally conscious tapestry.

2.4 The Technological Loom

Zara's commitment to innovation extends beyond design and production into the realm of technology. This section investigates the role of cutting-edge technologies, from AI-driven trend analysis to RFID tagging for inventory management. By embracing the digital loom, Zara not only stays ahead of industry trends but also enhances the customer experience. We unravel the threads of technological integration that have propelled Zara into the digital age.

2.5 Human Threads: Crafting a Creative Culture

Behind the seamless production processes and trendsetting designs are the people who breathe life into Zara's brand. Chapter 2 explores the unique culture within Zara, emphasizing collaboration, creativity, and a commitment to excellence. Weaving the human threads of Zara's success, we delve into the role of leadership, talent development, and employee empowerment in shaping the brand's innovative spirit.

As we untangle the intricate threads of innovation in Zara's design and production, Chapter 2 paints a vivid picture of a brand that not only anticipates trends but actively shapes them. Join us as we explore the dynamic interplay of creativity, technology, and human ingenuity that forms the very fabric of Zara's success.

3

The Marketplace Tapestry

Title: Beyond Borders: Zara's Global Expansion and Market Mastery

As the story of Zara unfolds, Chapter 3 illuminates the global tapestry woven by Amancio Ortega's strategic vision. From the local markets of La Coruña to the bustling streets of fashion capitals worldwide, Zara's journey of expansion and market dominance reflects a masterful understanding of global dynamics and consumer behavior.

3.1 Crossing Continents: Zara's Global Footprint

The journey of Zara from a small Spanish town to an international fashion giant is a testament to its successful global expansion strategy. Chapter 3 navigates through the milestones and challenges encountered as Zara ventured into diverse markets across Europe, Asia, the Americas, and beyond. We unravel the threads that allowed Zara to adapt to cultural nuances while maintaining a consistent brand identity.

3.2 The Supply Chain Symphony

Zara's ability to swiftly respond to changing fashion trends is intricately tied to its supply chain prowess. In this section, we dissect the supply chain orchestration that enables Zara to seamlessly move its creations from the drawing board to the storefront. We explore the delicate balance between centralized control and local responsiveness, revealing the key components that form the backbone of Zara's global market strategy.

3.3 Retail Revolution: Zara's Store as a Strategic Asset

Zara's retail stores are more than mere outlets; they are strategic assets in the brand's success. Chapter 3 examines how Zara's retail strategy, characterized by prime locations, unique store layouts, and interactive customer experiences, contributes to its market dominance. We unravel the threads of retail innovation that keep Zara at the forefront of the fashion retail landscape.

3.4 Digital Threads: E-Commerce and the Online Frontier

In the digital age, Zara has seamlessly integrated its online presence with its brick-and-mortar success. This section explores Zara's foray into e-commerce, its online marketing strategies, and the synergy between physical and digital retail channels. We unravel the digital threads that connect Zara to a global audience and analyze how technology has transformed the fashion retail landscape.

3.5 Navigating Trends: Zara's Adaptive Marketing

Marketing is the art of weaving stories, and Zara has mastered this art. Chapter 3 delves into Zara's marketing strategies, from its iconic word-of-mouth campaigns to social media dominance. We explore how Zara navigates the ever-changing landscape of consumer trends, remaining agile and relevant in an era of fast-paced digital communication.

As we explore the global marketplace tapestry woven by Zara, Chapter 3 offers a panoramic view of the brand's evolution from a local Spanish retailer to a global fashion phenomenon. Join us as we unravel the threads of Zara's global expansion, supply chain mastery, retail innovation, and adaptive marketing strategies.

4

The Customer Connection

Title: Tailoring Experiences: Zara's Customer-Centric Approach

In the rich fabric of Zara's success story, Chapter 4 delves into the crucial aspect of customer relations. Amancio Ortega's genius lies not only in creating trendsetting fashion but also in fostering a deep and enduring connection with the diverse clientele that walks through Zara's doors or shops online.

4.1 The In-Store Experience

Zara's brick-and-mortar stores are more than retail spaces; they are immersive environments carefully crafted to engage and captivate customers. This section explores the design philosophy behind Zara's stores, examining how the layout, ambiance, and visual merchandising contribute to a unique and compelling in-store experience. We unravel the threads of sensory appeal that make every visit to Zara a journey of discovery.

4.2 Fast Fashion, Personalized: Zara's Agile Merchandising

In the fast-paced world of fashion, Zara's ability to understand and respond to individual customer preferences is a defining feature. Chapter 4 investigates Zara's agile merchandising strategies, from limited-edition collections to responsive restocking. We explore how Zara tailors its offerings to meet the demands of diverse markets while maintaining a sense of exclusivity that resonates with customers.

4.3 Digital Dialogues: Zara's Online Community

As the digital realm becomes an integral part of the customer experience, Zara has embraced the power of online communities. This section analyzes Zara's digital engagement strategies, from social media interactions to user-generated content. We unravel the threads of the digital dialogues that strengthen the bond between Zara and its customers, turning them into active participants in the brand's narrative.

4.4 The Omnichannel Thread

In a world where customers seamlessly transition between online and offline channels, Zara's omnichannel strategy stands out. Chapter 4 explores how Zara integrates its physical and digital channels to provide a seamless and cohesive shopping experience. We unravel the omnichannel thread that connects Zara's diverse touchpoints, ensuring that the customer journey is not just a transaction but a holistic interaction.

4.5 Sustainable Style: Zara's Ethical Commitment

In an era where sustainability is a key concern for consumers, Zara has woven a thread of ethical commitment into its brand identity. This section explores Zara's initiatives in sustainable and ethical fashion, from eco-friendly materials to transparent supply chain practices. We unravel the threads of sustainability that align Zara with the values of a conscious consumer base.

Chapter 4 takes a magnifying glass to the threads of customer-centricity that run through Zara's success story. Join us as we explore the art of tailoring experiences, where each customer is not just a buyer but an integral part of the narrative that defines Zara's place in the global fashion landscape.

5

Chapter 5: Innovation and Adaptability: Zara's Enduring Legacy

Chapter 5: Innovation and Adaptability: Zara's Enduring Legacy

Title: Seamlessly Evolving: Zara's Culture of Innovation and Adaptability

In the final chapter of "Threads of Success," we unravel the enduring legacy of Zara by examining its culture of innovation and adaptability. Amancio Ortega's vision was not confined to a particular era or trend but was rooted in the ability to continuously innovate and adapt to the ever-changing dynamics of the fashion industry.

5.1 The Innovation Ecosystem

Zara's success is a testament to its relentless pursuit of innovation. Chapter 5 delves into the innovation ecosystem cultivated within Zara, exploring how the company fosters a culture that encourages experimentation and risk-taking. We unravel the threads of creativity that have led to breakthroughs in design, technology, and business processes, ensuring that Zara remains a trailblazer in the fashion world.

5.2 Learning from Data: Zara's Analytical Edge

Data-driven decision-making has become a cornerstone of success in the modern business landscape. This section explores how Zara leverages data analytics to understand market trends, consumer behavior, and operational efficiency. We unravel the threads of insights derived from data, showcasing how Zara's analytical edge contributes to its ability to stay ahead of the curve.

5.3 Adaptive Leadership: The Ortega Effect

Amancio Ortega's leadership style is a critical thread in Zara's success tapestry. This chapter investigates the leadership principles that have shaped Zara's culture, emphasizing adaptability, resilience, and a hands-on approach. We explore how Ortega's vision continues to inspire a new generation of leaders within Zara, ensuring that the company remains agile and responsive to challenges.

5.4 Future Threads: Zara's Vision Beyond

As we conclude our exploration, Chapter 5 looks toward the future threads that Zara is weaving. How is the brand positioning itself in the face of emerging trends, technological advancements, and shifting consumer expectations? We unravel the threads of Zara's vision for the future, examining its strategies for sustained success and continued relevance.

5.5 Lessons for Tomorrow

The final section reflects on the broader lessons that businesses, entrepreneurs, and enthusiasts can draw from Zara's remarkable journey. We unravel the universal threads of innovation, adaptability, and customer-centricity that transcend the fashion industry, offering insights that can inspire and guide those seeking to carve their path in the business world.

CHAPTER 5: INNOVATION AND ADAPTABILITY: ZARA'S ENDURING...

In "Seamlessly Evolving," Chapter 5 serves as a fitting conclusion to the exploration of Zara's success story. Join us as we unravel the threads that have made Zara not just a fashion icon but a symbol of enduring innovation and adaptability in the dynamic tapestry of the business world.

6

Threads of Reflection: Unraveling the Zara Phenomenon

Title: Legacy and Impact: Examining the Threads of Zara's Enduring Phenomenon

In this final chapter, we step back to reflect on the profound legacy and impact of Zara. From its humble beginnings to its global dominance, the Zara phenomenon has left an indelible mark on the fashion industry and business landscape. Chapter 6 invites readers to delve into the broader implications, cultural influence, and lasting lessons that the Zara success story imparts.

6.1 Cultural Influence: Zara's Impact on Fashion and Beyond

Zara's influence extends far beyond the world of fashion. This section explores how Zara has shaped and redefined consumer expectations, the fast-fashion model, and the very fabric of contemporary style. We unravel the threads of Zara's cultural impact, examining how it has influenced not only what we wear but also how we perceive and consume fashion in the 21st century.

6.2 Economic Implications: Zara's Contribution to Business Paradigms

Zara's success has not only transformed the retail industry but has also had broader economic implications. Chapter 6 investigates how Zara's business model, supply chain strategies, and market approach have influenced and disrupted traditional business paradigms. We unravel the economic threads of Zara's impact, from its contribution to the Spanish economy to its influence on global retail practices.

6.3 Lessons for Entrepreneurs: Unraveling the Entrepreneurial Threads

For aspiring entrepreneurs and business leaders, the Zara phenomenon offers a wealth of lessons. This section distills key entrepreneurial principles from Zara's journey, emphasizing innovation, adaptability, customer-centricity, and a forward-thinking approach. We unravel the threads of entrepreneurial wisdom that can inspire and guide those seeking to make their mark in the business world.

6.4 Ethical Considerations: Unraveling the Social Fabric

As the fashion industry grapples with ethical and sustainability concerns, Chapter 6 critically examines Zara's ethical considerations. We unravel the threads of Zara's social responsibility initiatives, exploring both its successes and challenges in fostering sustainable practices and responsible corporate citizenship.

6.5 Enduring Threads: Zara's Place in Business History

In the grand tapestry of business history, Zara stands as a unique and enduring thread. The final section of Chapter 6 reflects on Zara's place in the annals of business history, considering its legacy, the evolution of the fast-fashion landscape, and its enduring impact on the way businesses approach innovation, adaptability, and customer relations.

As we conclude our journey through the threads of Zara's success, Chapter 6 provides a comprehensive and reflective overview of the phenomenon that is Zara. Join us as we unravel the final threads that bind Zara's legacy to the broader tapestry of business and culture, leaving an imprint that will endure for generations to come.

7

Beyond the Seams: Charting the Future of Fashion and Business

Title: Innovations on the Horizon: Navigating the Future Threads of Success

In this forward-looking chapter, we turn our attention to the future of both the fashion industry and the broader business landscape. As Zara's story continues to unfold, Chapter 7 explores emerging trends, potential challenges, and the evolving dynamics that will shape the next chapters of success in the fast-paced world of fashion and commerce.

7.1 Technological Evolution: The Digital Tapestry

As technology advances, it inevitably transforms the way businesses operate. This section examines the role of cutting-edge technologies such as artificial intelligence, augmented reality, and blockchain in shaping the future of fashion and retail. We unravel the threads of technological evolution that will impact design processes, customer experiences, and supply chain management in the years to come.

7.2 Sustainability as Standard: Ethical Fashion on the Rise

The fashion industry is at a crossroads where sustainability is no longer a choice but a necessity. Chapter 7 explores how the future threads of success will be woven with a strong emphasis on ethical and sustainable practices. We unravel the growing importance of eco-friendly materials, circular fashion initiatives, and transparent supply chains in shaping the industry's landscape.

7.3 E-Commerce and the Shifting Retail Paradigm

As online shopping continues to surge, the traditional retail paradigm is undergoing a profound transformation. This section examines the evolving role of e-commerce, the integration of online and offline experiences, and the impact of digital marketplaces on consumer behavior. We unravel the threads of change in the retail landscape and how businesses can navigate the digital frontier.

7.4 Inclusivity and Diversity: Fashion for All

The fashion industry is increasingly recognizing the importance of inclusivity and diversity. Chapter 7 explores how the future of fashion will embrace a broader range of body types, ethnicities, and cultural influences. We unravel the threads of change in fashion representation, marketing strategies, and product offerings that reflect a more inclusive and diverse consumer base.

7.5 Lessons from Zara: Guiding Principles for the Future

As we peer into the future, this section reflects on the enduring lessons that businesses can draw from Zara's success story. We unravel the timeless principles of innovation, adaptability, customer-centricity, and ethical considerations that will remain crucial for businesses navigating the evolving landscape.

In Chapter 7, we gaze into the crystal ball of the business and fashion world, anticipating the future threads that will shape success. Join us as we explore the innovations, challenges, and guiding principles that will define the next era in the dynamic and ever-evolving realms of fashion and business.

8

A Tapestry Unfinished: Continuation of Zara's Journey

Title: Beyond Boundaries: Exploring New Horizons in the Ongoing Zara Legacy

In this concluding chapter, we continue the exploration of Zara's journey, recognizing that the tapestry of its success remains a work in progress. Chapter 8 delves into the ongoing evolution of Zara, addressing the brand's current endeavors, strategic expansions, and how it navigates the contemporary challenges and opportunities shaping the global business landscape.

8.1 Zara's Current Chapter: Recent Developments

This section provides an up-to-date analysis of Zara's recent initiatives, expansions, and notable achievements. We unravel the threads of the brand's present strategies, shedding light on its response to market dynamics, global events, and shifts in consumer behavior. By examining the latest chapters in Zara's story, we gain insights into its current standing in the competitive world of fashion and retail.

8.2 International Expansion and Market Penetration

As Zara continues to expand its global footprint, this section explores its recent forays into new markets and regions. We unravel the threads of international growth, examining how Zara tailors its strategies to suit diverse cultural landscapes and meet the demands of an ever-expanding and increasingly interconnected consumer base.

8.3 Challenges and Triumphs: Navigating the Competitive Landscape

In the fast-paced world of fashion, challenges and triumphs go hand in hand. This part of Chapter 8 unravels the threads of adversity and success, exploring how Zara addresses challenges such as changing consumer preferences, economic fluctuations, and increased competition. By examining how Zara adapts to and overcomes obstacles, we gain insights into the brand's resilience and strategic acumen.

8.4 Digital Frontiers: Zara in the Age of Connectivity

In an era of digital transformation, this section explores Zara's continued efforts to leverage technology and connectivity. We unravel the threads of Zara's digital strategies, online presence, and how it utilizes data-driven insights to enhance customer experiences, streamline operations, and stay at the forefront of the rapidly evolving digital landscape.

8.5 Future Prospects: The Uncharted Threads

As Zara steps into the future, this part of the chapter speculates on the potential directions the brand may take. We unravel the threads of future prospects, considering how Zara might further innovate, expand, and maintain its relevance in an ever-changing global marketplace. By examining the uncharted threads, we glimpse into the ongoing narrative of Zara's journey.

In the concluding chapter, we acknowledge that the story of Zara is one that continues to unfold. Join us as we explore the brand's present undertakings, recent triumphs, and future prospects, recognizing that the tapestry of Zara's success is a living narrative that weaves its way through the dynamic and unpredictable landscape of the business world.

9

Threads of Inspiration: Zara's Influence on Fashion and Business

Title: The Ripple Effect: Tracing Zara's Impact on the Industry

In this chapter, we delve into the broader impact of Zara on the fashion industry and business at large. As a pioneering force, Zara's success has set in motion a series of changes, innovations, and shifts that have resonated far beyond its own brand. Chapter 9 unravels the threads of inspiration woven by Zara, exploring its influence on industry practices, consumer expectations, and the entrepreneurial landscape.

9.1 Fast Fashion Revolution: Zara's Legacy in the Industry

Zara's adoption of the fast-fashion model revolutionized the industry. This section examines how Zara's success has influenced competitors, shaping the landscape of fashion retail. We unravel the threads of the fast-fashion revolution, exploring how other brands have sought to replicate Zara's agility and responsiveness in meeting consumer demands.

9.2 Supply Chain Innovations: Changing the Game

Zara's supply chain strategies have become a benchmark for efficiency and responsiveness. This part of the chapter delves into how Zara's supply chain innovations have influenced not only fashion but also other industries. We unravel the threads of supply chain management, exploring how businesses in various sectors have adopted similar principles to enhance their operational effectiveness.

9.3 Digital Transformation: Zara's Impact on Retail Technology

In the digital age, Zara's integration of technology into its business model has left an indelible mark. This section explores how Zara's approach to digital transformation has influenced the retail technology landscape. We unravel the threads of innovation in e-commerce, data analytics, and customer engagement, showcasing how Zara has spurred advancements in the way businesses leverage technology.

9.4 Consumer Expectations: Redefining the Shopping Experience

Zara's customer-centric approach has redefined expectations in the retail arena. This part of Chapter 9 explores how Zara's emphasis on agile merchandising, in-store experiences, and digital engagement has shaped consumer expectations. We unravel the threads of changing consumer behaviors, examining how other businesses are adapting to meet the evolving demands of the modern shopper.

9.5 Entrepreneurial Inspiration: Zara's Legacy for Business Leaders

Zara's journey is an inspiration for entrepreneurs and business leaders worldwide. This section delves into the entrepreneurial lessons that Zara's success story offers. We unravel the threads of innovation, adaptability, and risk-taking, examining how Zara has inspired a new generation of business leaders to approach challenges with a forward-thinking mindset.

Chapter 9 serves as a reflective exploration of Zara's influence on the broader landscape of fashion and business. Join us as we unravel the threads of inspiration that have emanated from Zara's success, tracing its impact on industry practices, technological advancements, consumer expectations, and the entrepreneurial spirit.

10

Threads of Continuity: Zara's Enduring Relevance

Title: Sustaining Success: The Evergreen Threads of Zara's Legacy

As we conclude our exploration of Zara's remarkable journey, Chapter 10 focuses on the enduring elements that have contributed to the brand's lasting success. This chapter delves into the timeless threads that continue to define Zara, examining the principles, values, and strategies that have allowed the brand to maintain its relevance in the face of evolving trends and a dynamic business landscape.

10.1 Core Principles: The Unchanging Threads

Zara's success is rooted in a set of core principles that have stood the test of time. This section explores the foundational threads that remain unchanged, from a commitment to innovation and quality to a relentless focus on customer satisfaction. We unravel the enduring principles that serve as the backbone of Zara's continued success.

10.2 Cultural Resilience: Adapting Without Compromise

As Zara expands globally, maintaining a strong organizational culture becomes crucial. This part of Chapter 10 examines how Zara has preserved its cultural identity while adapting to diverse markets and consumer preferences. We unravel the threads of cultural resilience, exploring how Zara fosters a sense of unity, innovation, and commitment among its teams worldwide.

10.3 Flexibility and Adaptability: The Agile Threads

Zara's ability to adapt swiftly to changing circumstances is a hallmark of its success. This section explores how Zara's agile approach extends beyond the design studio to its entire business model. We unravel the threads of flexibility and adaptability, examining how Zara remains responsive to market shifts, emerging trends, and unexpected challenges.

10.4 Customer-Centricity: The Enduring Connection

Zara's unwavering focus on the customer has been a key factor in its longevity. This part of the chapter explores how Zara maintains a deep and enduring connection with its customers, understanding their evolving needs and preferences. We unravel the threads of customer-centricity that continue to drive Zara's success in an increasingly competitive market.

10.5 Legacy in Leadership: Passing Down the Threads

As leadership transitions occur, the legacy of Zara is passed down through the threads of leadership principles and values. This section explores how Zara ensures continuity in leadership, passing on the visionary mindset that has defined the brand from its inception. We unravel the threads of leadership legacy that contribute to the brand's enduring success.

In this final chapter, we unravel the threads of continuity that have allowed

Zara to sustain its success over the years. Join us as we explore the timeless principles, cultural resilience, adaptability, customer-centricity, and leadership legacy that form the fabric of Zara's enduring relevance in the ever-evolving landscape of fashion and business.

11

Threads of Reflection: Lessons and Insights from Zara's Journey

Title: Weaving Wisdom: Reflecting on the Threads of Zara's Odyssey

In this reflective chapter, we step back to distill the essential lessons, insights, and wisdom gleaned from Zara's extraordinary journey. Chapter 11 serves as a synthesis of the key principles, strategies, and cultural nuances that have contributed to Zara's success, offering a tapestry of knowledge for business leaders, entrepreneurs, and enthusiasts alike.

11.1 The Power of Innovation: Weaving a Culture of Creativity

At the heart of Zara's success lies a relentless commitment to innovation. This section reflects on the transformative power of innovation, exploring how Zara fosters a culture of creativity that permeates every aspect of the business. We unravel the threads of inventive thinking, strategic experimentation, and the importance of staying at the forefront of industry trends.

11.2 Adaptability as a Strategic Imperative: Navigating Change with Grace

Zara's ability to adapt swiftly has been a linchpin in its resilience. This part of Chapter 11 reflects on the strategic imperative of adaptability, examining how Zara navigates change with grace, whether in response to market trends, technological shifts, or global events. We unravel the threads of flexibility that allow Zara to remain agile in a dynamic business landscape.

11.3 The Customer-Centric Paradigm: Tailoring Experiences for Success

Zara's unwavering customer focus has been instrumental in its longevity. This section reflects on the customer-centric paradigm, exploring how Zara tailors experiences to meet and exceed customer expectations. We unravel the threads of customer engagement, feedback utilization, and the pivotal role of understanding and connecting with the target audience.

11.4 Balancing Tradition and Modernity: Crafting a Timeless Legacy

Zara's success is marked by a harmonious blend of tradition and modernity. This part of Chapter 11 reflects on the art of balancing timeless principles with contemporary strategies, examining how Zara has crafted a legacy that transcends eras. We unravel the threads of heritage, acknowledging the importance of respecting roots while embracing the demands of the present and future.

11.5 Leadership Wisdom: Passing Down the Threads of Vision

Leadership within Zara has been characterized by a visionary mindset. This section reflects on the leadership wisdom emanating from Zara's journey, exploring how visionary leaders shape and sustain success. We unravel the threads of leadership legacy, acknowledging the role of inspired guidance in steering a brand toward enduring prosperity.

In Chapter 11, we weave together the threads of wisdom extracted from Zara's journey. Join us as we reflect on the enduring principles of innovation, adaptability, customer-centricity, the delicate balance of tradition and modernity, and the leadership legacy that together form the fabric of Zara's unique and lasting success story.

12

Threads of Inspiration: Charting Your Own Success

Title: Unleashing Potential: Drawing Lessons from Zara's Threads of Success

As we conclude our exploration of Zara's journey, Chapter 12 serves as a call to action, encouraging readers to draw inspiration from the threads of success woven by Zara. This chapter provides a roadmap for individuals, entrepreneurs, and businesses to apply the lessons learned from Zara's remarkable story and craft their own path to success.

12.1 Embracing a Culture of Innovation: Nurturing Creative DNA

This section encourages readers to embrace a culture of innovation within their own endeavors. By drawing inspiration from Zara's commitment to creativity, readers can cultivate an environment that fosters inventive thinking, experimentation, and a forward-looking mindset. We unravel the threads of innovation, urging individuals and businesses to weave their own tapestry of creative success.

12.2 Agility and Adaptability: Navigating Change with Confidence

Reflecting on Zara's adaptability, this part of Chapter 12 emphasizes the importance of agility in the face of change. Readers are encouraged to develop a strategic imperative for adaptability, responding to shifts in their respective industries with confidence and resilience. We unravel the threads of flexibility, urging individuals and businesses to navigate change with grace.

12.3 Customer-Centric Strategies: Building Lasting Connections

The customer-centric paradigm is a key takeaway from Zara's success. This section prompts readers to prioritize understanding and connecting with their audience, tailoring experiences to meet evolving expectations. We unravel the threads of customer engagement, urging individuals and businesses to build lasting connections that go beyond transactions.

12.4 Balancing Tradition and Innovation: Crafting a Timeless Legacy

Acknowledging the balance of tradition and modernity in Zara's success, this part of Chapter 12 encourages readers to carve their own legacy by respecting heritage while embracing contemporary strategies. We unravel the threads of balancing tradition and innovation, urging individuals and businesses to craft a timeless legacy that reflects their unique identity.

12.5 Leadership Vision: Inspiring Success Through Guiding Principles

Reflecting on the leadership wisdom from Zara's journey, this section encourages individuals to embrace a visionary mindset in their leadership roles. By passing down guiding principles and inspiring success, readers can shape the trajectory of their endeavors. We unravel the threads of leadership legacy, urging individuals to lead with vision and purpose.

In Chapter 12, we invite readers to actively engage with the lessons learned from Zara's success. Join us as we explore the practical application of innovation, adaptability, customer-centricity, the delicate balance of tradition and modernity, and leadership legacy in your own journey to unleash potential and chart a path to success.

13

Summary

"Threads of Success: Unraveling the Business Genius of Amancio Ortega and Zara" is a comprehensive exploration of Zara's journey from a small Spanish town to a global fashion powerhouse. The book comprises twelve chapters, each focusing on a different aspect of Zara's success. Here is a summarized overview of the key themes:

Chapters 1-2: The Foundation of Success
　These chapters delve into the early life of Amancio Ortega, the founder of Zara, and the foundational principles that shaped the brand's identity. Emphasis is placed on the innovative business model that combines speed, flexibility, and a vertically integrated supply chain.

Chapters 3-5: Global Expansion and Market Mastery
　The book explores Zara's global footprint, supply chain orchestration, retail strategies, and its successful integration of online and offline channels. It also examines how Zara navigates trends, adapts marketing strategies, and establishes a strong presence in the global marketplace.

Chapters 6-8: The Customer Connection and Ongoing Legacy
　These chapters focus on Zara's customer-centric approach, examining the in-store experience, agile merchandising, and digital engagement. Chapter

8 looks toward the future, exploring Zara's current endeavors, recent developments, and strategic expansions.

Chapters 9-11: Industry Influence and Enduring Relevance

These chapters reflect on Zara's broader impact on the fashion industry, its supply chain innovations, and its influence on retail technology. Chapter 10 explores the enduring elements of Zara's success, emphasizing core principles, cultural resilience, adaptability, customer-centricity, and leadership legacy.

Chapter 12: Inspiration for the Future

The final chapter serves as a call to action, encouraging readers to draw inspiration from Zara's success. It provides a roadmap for individuals and businesses to apply the lessons learned, focusing on innovation, adaptability, customer-centric strategies, balancing tradition and innovation, and leadership vision.

In summary, "Threads of Success" weaves a comprehensive narrative that not only chronicles Zara's rise to prominence but also extracts valuable lessons and insights applicable to a broad spectrum of industries. It serves as a source of inspiration for those looking to navigate the complexities of business with agility, innovation, and a deep commitment to customer satisfaction.